"Life never takes its boot off the accelerator, regardless of what's going on around the world. In Victor Clevenger's *The Most Beautiful Thing About June,* he demonstrates this amid a divided country and a global pandemic. From gritty poems about sacrifice, morality and dysfunctional relationships, this punchy collection is a reminder that as life speeds ahead, all you can do is hang on."

— **Cord Moreski**, author of *The News Around Town*

"Victor Clevenger's latest release, "The Most Beautiful Thing About June" features 25 poems that knock you out cold, and when you come to they do it all over again. This collection of poems is carefully crafted from Clevenger's own blood, pain, and experiences which lend clarity to the authenticity and sincerity of his storytelling ability as he navigates the world. This collection is only a small peak into the world of a truly important writer."

— **Tohm Bakelas**, poet/editor of *Between Shadows Press*

The Most Beautiful Thing About June

Victor Clevenger

ISBN: 9798367085426

Cover art design: Cody Sexton

Grateful acknowledgment is given to *Big Hammer, Full of Crow, Rusty Truck, The Lunch Bucket Brigade, Live Nude Poems, Chiron Review, 48th Street Press, Horror Sleaze Trash, The Assylum Floor,* and *River Dog* where some of these poems first appeared in various forms.

*for all my dear friends who are going insane but still
surviving these crazy days we are living in.*

i love you all.

TABLE OF CONTENTS

About the Author

WAR

walking through the front door late again
& my daughter was making dinner for all her
siblings   macaroni with cheese & tuna fish
canned peas & bread with butter
i sat down & she put a full plate in front of me
i thanked her but stood up & gave her my seat
telling her go ahead & eat while it's hot   i'll wait
opening a beer & searching out the pile of mail
she shouts that the mailbox was empty today
so i walk back & stand in the doorway
thinking about my life at her age   in 1998
when i cut a piece of cake on my nineteenth
birthday she was just five-days old & still adjusting
to the ever-changing contours of the crooks in my
arms   so much has changed with time
she has grown into a young woman whose heart
beats hot even in the cold air of responsibilities
she keeps selflessness warm enough to survive
& i'm goddamn proud of her   but wonder
if she'd feel the same way about me if she knew
that i have written more suicide notes than i can
count   all in attempts to find the words that i feel
are right words that she'll understand   words that
won't require sleepless nights   words that won't
make her feel fucked up words that won't make
her want to break the glass in every framed picture
of me when the war between her good   & the bad
that i'll leave behind begins

FROM A BLACK ACE BOOK TO THE PEARLY GATES

it's something the great creator
finally got right

joey, thank you for reminding us all

that not even death
can mar the beauty in the wings
of a butterfly

POEM FOR A NEW GENERATION OF WHITE SHEET WEARERS

licking the dried blood & pride
from your grandfather's cheek bones
does not make you tough
it just leaves a bad taste lingering
on your ignorant tongue

that you'll one day have to cut out
of your own mouth
if you ever desire
to passionately kiss the soft lips
of forgiveness

WHEN THE MUSIC STOPS

sing a song about common sense
bouncing around in spaces filled with lots
or less than lots

sing a song about how you dream a future to be

how a neck feels a beat of a pulsing heart

how a hummingbird looks big
to a grounded honeybee

nighttime becomes a daytime for a moon

a lion & a bullet lunging for the flesh incite last
words

soldiers in wars hold ice cubes
like pieces of treasure

like peace treaties that melt down fingertips

like disappearing ink from a child's trick bag
that could never produce a signature
on a dotted line

sing a song

about how a long kiss from a stranger can birth
a spooky familiarity to a summer fling
that ended in September

sing a song

about how outlaws tough as nails still wrote love
letters but never sent them

sing a song

& even if nothing more
than a damned hot breath exhaled noise
emits from your mouth

sing

that song

SOME PEOPLE WEAR THE SHARK'S TOOTH AROUND THEIR NECK TO SHOW STRENGTH & MASCULINITY

for lester madden

in death you showed them all

that you were the toughest son-of-a-bitch
in the allegheny cemetery

buried

with the whole shark's head on top
of your bones

I Will Never Know Why

a young woman
holding a red rose
like a magic wand
on a pittsburgh street corner
needs $5 to feel satisfied

ABYSS

our life repeats
day after day
after day driving
dirty highways
misfortune blows kisses
a black car
broken down
abandoned on a side road
with no spark in her plugs
sitting there cold
& motionless
mimics
you well

POEM ABOUT A SAD-EYED BOY

drinking whiskey

like his father & crying

like his mother

he threw up

on the bathroom floor

all alone

SPARCE PLEASURES

the shoulders of a city throbbing
machinery oil down a back
smoke brushes above the eyes
of another day

like years ago
i remember my father
returning home from work & sitting
his lunch pail on the countertop
to discard the trash

usually just wadded plastic
sandwich bags but some days
there would be small pieces
of potato chips or a quarter stick
of a peanut butter snack bar

that my sisters & i would race for
to be the winner & have
the first begging fingers stretched out
before him as if he were handing out

tiny pieces of his heart

His Left Shoe Saved Him

when he was 14, a woman asked him to pull his
socks up & his underwear down. he did it. he didn't
argue with her; there was no pushing, pulling, or
compromise. he didn't feel dirty about it. he didn't
feel victimized, he just

leaned forward at the waist & tugged on the first sock
as she reached out with every single finger she had &
ran them through his greasy hair. he stayed down
there. he held the 'touch my toes' pose & tugged on
the other sock;

they were both white, his underwear was white, & his
biggest fear was the light of day shining through the
window, because he knew the possibility was great
that by 4 o'clock in the afternoon on the days after
his mother

would bring home leftovers from the town pavilion
food court, that there would be shit stains in the
fabric. the only thing that saved his dignity was the
fact that she wanted the radio turned on for the sound,
so as she went to turn

the dial, he quickly stripped his underwear off &
shoved them deep into the toe of his tennis shoe. she
came back into the room to find him just how she
requested. she was happy. she was 29 & he had no
goddamn clue how to

begin making love to her & when she asked him what

he liked the most he just laid down on his back &
smiled. he didn't know what he liked back then, but
she gave him plenty to choose from & they were all
better choices than

the familiar squeeze-n-rub of his thumb & fingers
under the blankets as his older brother snored out
another drunk on the brass trundle bed.

STRAY PUSSY IN TALL GRASS

on the side of a collapsing shed sat three metal
chairs, painted many times over the years, brown
green blues all rusted & peeling exposing layers of
days that died long before this one.

one afternoon a drifter cat stretched out across the
flat of a chair, its face the color of wood ash & it
stood tall upon approach before crouching down
into a wary posture, a hiss with a hint of menace,
it's okay stray pussy was whispered & the cat left
undisturbed while hands grabbed a hold of the
remaining two chairs.

screams developed quickly as dozens of bees flew
out of the tall grass, from below the chairs & waged
war. they were ruthless, thrusting stingers like
swords through tender flesh from ankles to armpits.

the chairs were swung wildly & released, tossed
away to run in retreat & that old bastard man stood
next door on the front lawn laughing until he
coughed, choking on a mouthful of tobacco juices
causing him spit it all onto the ground. looking back
towards the chairs i saw the cat running away,
scooting underneath the bottom of a fence.

there was no way to tell if the cat was stung, but the
bee stings from ankle to armpit swole, were as large
as a half-dollar coin, were sore but survivable.

later that day while riding a bicycle across town,
before sundown, that drifter cat was stretched out in
the middle of the road a few blocks away. initial

thought from a distance was smashed flat & dead,
but it wasn't smashed flat or dead at all, it was just
stretched out enjoying the end of a painful day

& i guess there isn't much that's wrong with that.

FROM EXPERIENCE

poems about wine
about beer bottles
about waking drunk with deborah sue
about fucking a mistress in a car
about smoking expensive things
about smoking cheap things
about waking to fire in a bedroom & losing
    everything you owned
about a grandmother's broken leg
    from falling on ice
about a car crash on i-70
about a mother uniting races
about a sister uniting sexes
about days in prison
about nights in prison
about trips to watertown, ny
about being used by a father
about a summer living inner city
about a summer living rural
about poison ivy on your cock
about packing fruit in a produce warehouse
    at 5:30 saturday mornings
about pissing kidney stones in 2004
about seven stitches in your head in 2007
about a neighbor hanging himself from the rafters
    in his garage
are all relatable to far too many people
it's the love poems that are not   i guess

SEXUAL SEASONS

we bitch about how beauty loses its luster
within the added layers of comfort

i tell you about how
i've not seen the marks
that stretch across this city's stomach in weeks

then you say screw you october & november
& december

& i say screw you january & february too

it's march thru september that we love

when the cold winds refuse to blow every day
down the boulevards we travel

like wild animals

chasing

each other

SHE HAD NEVER TRIED WINE

tried it for the first time on the night
that she crossed the line with me
she felt so sexy in her panties
bought for the occasion
but her stomach ached after half a bottle
passed through her lips
i pounded down a bottle & a half of red
like it was cold milk
at a ghost pepper eating contest
she tried to be motionless
said the room was rotating through her eyes
concentrated on the ceiling fan far above her head
my hot-drunk-breath penetrated
the lace & rhinestones
her breath was deep
suddenly pushed me off of her
kicked her feet around under the bed sheets
but she was trapped   it took effort
she finally kicked herself free
rolled to her right & upchucked
over the side of the bed
how'd you stomach that vile stuff   she asked
wiping her weeping eyes & burning nostrils
i drink it nightly like it's a stress remedy
a good escape from my shitty life
well. i. am. not. ever. drinking. that. stuff. again.
that's fine   i said
just clean that mess up
i was still horned up
& hard as the handle on a lath hammer
but knew i would shrivel up
just as soon as she got that smell swirling
be a gentleman & clean it for me

she said
i don't feel good
i don't care   i replied
it's your mess & you clean it
i'm not doing it
do it   i replied again as i raised
my hand into the air with tipsy exclamation
she shouted
you. wanna. threaten. me. you. son-of-a-bitch.
swung her fist & struck me in the nose
that fist took me by surprise
it bloodied my face
i looked just as horrible as she did now
we laughed
once her drunk ass passed out
i cleaned everything up & watched the clock
waiting for the right time to wake her up
& kick her out
eight o'clock was the time i chose
i woke her   but i startled her
she swung an elbow this time & bloodied me again
she was one of the worst nights i've had
with a woman
but goddamn she was beautiful
on our second date
we just stuck to beer

COLOR ME CONFUSION

yellow gave orange a peppermint kiss
& afterwards orange closed the window

yellow went back home to his purple lover
he was singing   seven nation army
& he had to pass a wal-mart
so he stopped to buy a new notebook
his shoes got wet from puddles in the parking lot

across town   green watched the streetlight
cut through the damp tree branches

& red   he walked through the church doors
fell to his knees & sobbed for blue

blue had turned black with cancer months
ago & brittled like rose potpourri petals

pink walked through the door & embraced red
whispering to him   gray works in mysterious
ways

brown bought a fifth of whiskey & a lotto ticket as
white waited for him at home with a pork chop
dinner & a confetti cake that says
happy anniversary

& i   i sit here   still having no clue how to do this
new style of math that my 5th grader
brings home every night

♂PUMPING ɓASOLINE

in a sinclair parking lot
a kid that looked like daniel radcliffe
asked me   what's the best thing
about the prison guard life

looked down & realized i was still
in uniform.

he said   i don't know if i could do it
you're pretty fucking crazy aren't you
they do crazy things in there don't they
make the new guys suck dicks   don't they
you ever seen someone sucking dick in there
i have an uncle doing a five-year sentence
maybe you know him   he's a creep
likes to bang heroin & meth-head chicks
according to the court documents
bought from an undercover
i remember one time he left me
at the neighbor's house   went to get high
& i got bit on the leg by their dog
my old man was pissed   threatened to kill
my uncle   they haven't talked since
in a way i feel that it is all my fault

a redheaded woman walked out the store
across the parking lot

that's my mom   the kid said
i gotta go

she smiled
climbed into a chevy cavalier

& drove away

i finished pumping my gas
went home

& changed clothes

THE DIRTY SHIRT

looking out a kitchen window towards
a mid-day sky before a sunday storm
in september & it reminds me of the color
of a soiled t-shirt that i'd tossed
into a washing machine yesterday
worn by my seven-year-old daughter
in the backyard
playing carelessly with no expressed concern
that wet dirt & dried ashes being smeared
into the fibers may never release
to reveal the intended colors of the thick threads
eighteen-dollars such a waste
i think to myself as the wind blows stronger
& a small squirrel runs from one tree to another
taking a crooked path
the first raindrop hits the glass
& i give up on the thought of walking outside
to pick up the shovel from the vegetable garden
instead i walk into an empty living room
& turn on the television to hear
that the storm should over by dinnertime
& that's fine but honestly i wouldn't care
if it rained until morning because now
my daughter will beg to go outside before bedtime &
i'll tell her no it's still wet
& you'll ruin another shirt
unless you wear the one that you ruined yesterday
& she'll think hard about the choice
& voice her concerns
but it won't go the way she hopes that it will
to wear a different shirt
& she'll start to cry
& i'll be the mean one

who never lets her do anything fun
like play in the wet dirt & ashes
because i care more about her shirt than i do
about her happiness
& that's far from the truth
but try
to get her to believe that

ℰXPOSED

three-nineteen in the morning and nobody sleeps. she
is bleeding from between her legs, & i am bleeding
from behind my eyes. we are ok. it's normal
happenings; it's clotting, & cramping, & predictable
— she is a woman with the entire

ensemble of woman parts, & has a few nights like
this around the first of the month — i am a man who
is trying to survive in this world with only his words.
we both sit & experience small pieces of our insides
dying in cycles & passing. she

shoves, & presses cotton. i type my thoughts on a
machine that is missing the 'T' button, but i just press
really hard where it used to sit, & it works from time
to time. when it doesn't work i shout. she wears
heavy laced panties to hold the cotton in place.

when the cotton gets full & fails; when her lace soils
& stains she shouts too. there are times we shout
together, but when we don't shout, & she is not
shoving or pressing, & i am not pressing either, we
sit beside each other & listen to the sounds

in the darkness of this apartment: ceiling fans
humming, heavy refrigerator motors buzzing,
aquarium bubbles popping, soft thumping steps in the
stairwell, air conditioners blowing, & the neighbors'
moans — some moans peak interest, some moans

sound like murder; they are all a muse when i sit

down to type, & yes, there is a possibility that she
may not be amused when she reads this, & sees that i
have exposed pieces of her, but i guess that is the
result of choosing to die in cycles with me.

bloody night after bloody night.

IT'S UNDERSTANDABLE

the choice was work on time this morning or staying
in bed & trying to put myself inside of her. i had
been up since 5 a.m. sitting at the edge of the bed
smoking cigarettes & watching strangers pull in &
out of the parking lot through the open venetians.

her nipples were sore from baby suckling; her eyes
were blood sprinkled from rest-lacked nights, but her
sacrifices willing to give me a moment on this chilly,
early fall morning. finish that cigarette first, she said
turning over & pulling the extra blankets over her
head.

i finished the cigarette & crawled back across the bed
to her side, anticipation already had me on the verge
of hard, & i fought her tight grip to pull the blankets
back from her head. i gave up & just kissed her
knuckles that were exposed, compassion &
understanding.

i'm gonna be late, i told her as i climbed out of bed &
put on my jacket, zipping it up, i reached down &
zipped my pants up as well.

saturday morning & the moment had passed as the
church bells down the street rang 6 a.m. & the radio
disc jockey yammered, what happened to
summertime anyway?

SECOND EXCERPT FROM THE FOXES

lora kisses me on the cheek
i look over her shoulder
out the window

i can see a flashing red sign again
& two foxes standing
underneath it

everything seems to blend with the reflection
of her & i   we step left   they step left
the foxes mimic our movements
my hand
          on lora's shoulder
i try to turn her around
so that she can see the happenings
but she refuses

*

she asks me if i ever regret
that she was the girl who took my virginity

that sometimes she worries

imagines herself to be a thief
taking something she can never give back
moments   fleeting thoughts
most days knowing the maps that lead

to the buried pieces of treasures in her mind
were burnt years ago

& the ashes

tossed into the mouth of the ghost
of teen spirit

*

i tell her it was a gift
to never worry about it
that the lives we now live
give us more important things
to worry about

like keeping the neon signs that sits above
our designated plots in the boneyard
flashing the word

u n o c c u p i e d

*

she stops talking   steps to the side of me
i take a small step away from her to get
a better look through the window

one fox in the reflection turns its head

the other one disappears
i turn quickly & lora is gone too

i say her name

she doesn't reply

                                         *

eyes closed i shout loudly
believing she will feel the vibrations of my chords
in deep places

a voice responds but it's not her voice
i open my eyes & a man driving a car
asks me to please stop shouting

buckled tightly into the backseat
i wiggle like a moth trying
to exit the squeeze of a damp cocoon

i ask him   where are we going
as he looks into the mirror making eye contact

such a large face
intimidating   but jovial
driving with only one hand on the steering wheel

                                         *

knocking on your screen door

good with prine   he asks
turning up the volume

sure   i say   & ask once again
where are we going

looking ahead through the windshield
i see a sign that says   TUNNEL

*

everything goes dim as we enter

car tires hum

& the strong smell
of potatoes frying in grease enters my nose

i close my eyes
& inhale

*

car brakes squeals
glass breaks shatters after thunderous sound

a sudden feeling in my mouth
like a clump of clipped hair had been shoved
through my lips

i open my eyes and quickly spit
falling forward
no longer cocooned
no longer a backseat passenger
no longer a jovial face staring back in the mirror

i'm airborne feet above head
arms stretched fingertips touching pavement dragging

i feel tiny pebbles lodging into crevices underneath
my fingernails

they start to tear loose

as my body completes its rotation
i stop

a broken man

                                        *

awoken by a strange voice

rolling to the right
a large fish aquarium sits against a wall &
a clothes dryer sits in a corner of a room
that looks exactly like my room
when i was fourteen

the back bedroom of my grandmother's house
reminiscent of a morning waking
with bloodshot eyes

from a st. patrick's day drunk
the night before

i listen for the voice again
it get louder as the door begins to open

hello   a short man dressed like a doctor says
          you're lucky to be alive

we found you just in time

                                        *

sore but alright
          trying to sit up

two foxes entered the room in nurse scrubs
suggesting that it was not wise for me
to do so   as they wheeled an old television strapped
to a cart into the room

it looked like something i remember seeing
in elementary school

i've got to go   i shouted

but they never acknowledged me

climbing out of the bed
i opened the door
but there was no hallway
only red shrubs & a picture window

two men stood on the other side
angry

thrusting their pointed fingers
at the empty space
in front of them

ᴄHAPPY ᴄHOUR

blue silk. he wore his shirt with the top two buttons
undone & had suspenders to hold his pants up. He
looked like mork in business casual, shaking the seat
of the barstool a few times before pulling it over onto
its side. he placed it back upright & shook it once
more before sitting down on it. do you remember that
black barstool, the broken one?

i remember it, his friend said, you are the son-of-a-
bitch who broke it. christ, i crashed straight down
onto my ass when that thing broke. for a second i
thought you had broken your back. no. i was okay,
he laughed, but the fall left the biggest bruise on me
for two weeks. do you know how strange my ex-wife
looked at me when i stripped down

naked in front of her? it looked like an elephant's
trunk had been sucking on my ass cheek, i mean, it
looked like a purple hickey, a goddamn eggplant, or
something. they both laughed again, slurped the
foam from the top of their brews. happy hour & a
woman across the room dripped mustard from her
sandwich, it landed right where her left

breast was. quickly, she eyed the room to see if
anyone had noticed that smearing it with a napkin
only made it worse. from where i sat, it looked as if
she had taken a bullet into the heart. weeping yellow
blood, her cotton shirt absorbed it, expanded it wide
like a last sunflower blooming amongst masses of the
dead on an early kansas morning.

SMOKE & KNUCKLES

one hot july weekend underneath a bridge where
crumbling concrete had been tagged & retagged
with spray paints like you'd see on a rusted-out box
car in the boneyard was a marijuana paradise where
fish & frogs swam in water that would reach up to
the neck of most men.

reggie said a guy with a sublime sun tattoo laughed
out loud when a crooked stick floated past looking
like a snake making sudden jerkish moves. a girl
shrieked freaked, ran out of the water quickly,
stumbled fell & when her top came off her
breasts were exposed.

her boyfriend who looked more like joe buck than
joe rogan wasn't amused at all when a stranger said,
yeah shake 'em baby, so a black eye was served
with one punch. the girl started shouting at her
boyfriend to stop, voice shrill undertone anger but
her joe threw a few more

punches until she grabbed him by the hair &
tugged. he stopped, told her it was all for her that no
son-of-a-bitch would disrespect her as long as he was
around. she blushed smiled & her anger retreated
like the black eye guy. reggie said throughout the
scuffle he kept his mouth shut

while staring at the girl's wet hair, trash bag black
shining in the sun & her nipples he said were both
pierced . . . affixed to the barrels were
hummingbirds that bounced up & down with her
excitement. he said it was a damn-fine-beautiful
thing to see three o'clock on a saturday afternoon

& that it was a damn-fine-beautiful thing to think
about three o'clock on a sunday morning as wind
shook the walls of a small tent, blowing dirt through
the tattered seams to the point where he could feel
grit sitting on his lips when he pressed them
together like a rough kiss that

he had no desire for, so he packed his things into his
car & drove the seven miles back to his apartment
building smoking a cigarette & wondering if the
hummingbird girl remembers any of the unfamiliar
faces in yesterday's crowd, more specifically, just
his.

AND THIS IS WHO WE FEAR

death has a big picture rolodex
& blisters on his fingertips from spinning it
it always makes the same sound

swoosh...tisk tisk tisk....tisk tisk...tisk.......tisk

it stops & then he plucks the card out
reads the name
combs his silver-thinned hair
ties his shoelaces
rubs the broad shoulders of his live-in
kisses her cheek
then heads off to work

death has a lover?

of course   & i find it odd too
that death has a broad-shouldered
normal looking woman
i mean   come on   it's death
a real bad boy that should be pulling the hottest lays
that you & i could only dream about pulling
& yet he chooses normal

maybe after his rough goings at the office
pulling double shifts while working
the weekends weekdays & holidays
his normal woman is a calm beautiful to him

maybe it is her simplicity that gets him off—
her shoulder length brown hair & soft groomed
fingernails

or maybe he has just ran himself bored
with the hot lays in his youth
& this one now keeps him straight

death is centuries old
& will tell you   i have trouble these days seeing
the differences in oranges & onions
but she peels them for me now & slices them neatly

with that confession   i am now convinced

that it is just the fact that she cares
when most all the other people tremble at his
presence

i am death   he says to her
as they sit beside each other on the sofa

who is going to kill me when i can't do this anymore

you will always do it darling   she tells him each
time
the topic surfaces

you did it way before i existed
& you will take me one day
then find another woman to pass time with
i know this & have come to accept it

AH   GODDAMN   CURSE IT   he shouts

but sweetheart   she replies
rubbing death's hand & fingers

you know   he says
i found a gut-shivering admiration
for the old bastard that i took last week

he climbed up under a bridge
with a bottle of gin & suicided
it wasn't a sloppy one this time   i kept it decent
he didn't even shit his pants

you liked that   she asks still rubbing

i really liked it   death mumbles

the doorbell rings & they ignore it
it rings again & death tells her
just see who it is & tell them that i am throat-deep
in the washtub

she stops rubbing   stands up   & goes to the door

it's hank

want to play some pinochle   hank asks her

she shouts to death   HONEY, IT'S HANK
he wants to know if you want to play some pinochle

pinochle   i'm in the water   remember

oh i'm sorry hank   she says
i forgot that he is throat-deep in the washtub
maybe we can get together another time

another time   hank says
yes another time   she tells him

sure   hank says

& she shuts the door
walks back to the sofa
sits down

rubs some more
& starts whistling

i don't play pinochle   death tells her

i don't either   she stops whistling & tells him
cheer up   you are going to live forever
& nobody else can say that

OH THAT SOUNDS MISERABLE   death shouts
my legs feel like withered carrots already
i can't take this anymore   TRY TO KILL ME

OH I COULD NEVER   she sobs

death stands up casually
then dashes & hurdles himself towards the open
window

she sobs louder

death falls four floors into the yellow petals
of a forsythia bush

she stands four floors above him at the window
shouting

YOU DID THIS LAST WEEK & POKED YOUR
EYE REMEMBER   COME BACK UPSTAIRS

death stands up
brushes his shirt sleeves & trousers off
hangs his head
& stares at the laces of his shoes

as he maneuvers the stairs back up to the fourth floor
there is dirty green carpet in the hallways

he opens the door squinting & blinking
AH IT'S HORRIBLE   he hollers defeated

did you poke it again   she asks him

twice   he tells her   once with the bush
& once with my finger

why with your finger   she asks

i never saw it coming   he replies

well you are still alive   she smiles
as she walks over & locks the window down

death rubs an ice cube against his eyes
& they sit back down on the sofa

she rubs again too
rubs his hand a little bit harder this time

he was sore but tolerated it

the forsythia bush
          didn't survive

ITCHY EYELIDS

he woke confused   laid out on the ground
with his finger shoved inside his nose
he wakes that way at times in the early mornings
with it shoved up there real deep   so his finger
was not what caused his confusion when he woke

the woman sitting beside him was the creator of it
all . . .

christ   you're an ugly thing   she said   did i
screw you   you are naked   i really hope that we
didn't screw each other because you look just like
my grandfather?
but not the way he looks today
or the way that he looked yesterday
you look like he did
when he was thirty-five years old
he had six toes on one foot & a pet monkey
i swear to you that he did
i have a picture of him somewhere in my purse
have you seen my purse

no   he said   have you seen my pants
standing up & grabbing an empty milk carton
from a small pile of trash that was beside him
he tugged on the sealed ends of the cardboard
to spread them apart   he reached down
with his hand & grabbed his testicles
shoved them with his penis inside the carton

she laughed & asked why

it's all that i have   he said   my pants are gone

right   she said   oh look
i found my purse

do you still want to see that picture of my
grandfather

THE MOST BEAUTIFUL THING ABOUT JUNE

well   shitface   anger is a heavy anchor
it is tied to the toes of every man
& i have watched far too many fools drown
before they found the ability to simply
untie the knot
& breathe comfortably again

i'm not angry   or drowning   i'm simply
just saying that you are eighty-four pounds now
& not beautiful anymore

you promised that i would always
be beautiful in your eyes   lee
you're a real son-of-a-bitch!
you really are

june   when we met
you were a child's handful under two-seventy
& it worked

you're a pig

well   i liked you better that way   june
you were once big & beautiful
your weight felt good when we fucked
it was comforting

i'm beautiful now!

look   june   i left the car running
& you are working the only open aisle in the store
it's eight o'clock & there are people in this line

behind me   i'll just leave

just stand over by the door   lee
i'll take care of the people quickly
& then we can talk

lee walked over by the door
& leaned against one of the gumball machines
there were three machines
they were all red machines
the balls inside were all pink

the man that had been standing in line behind lee
was wearing a gray t-shirt   deep v-necked
& his chest hair stuck outside of the neckline
like spider legs
it was thick like a bird's nest

the man standing behind him
had a narrow mustache
that was poorly trimmed
& he wore a full-necked shirt
the shirt was white
his mustache was brown
& he touched the shoulders of the man
with a gray t-shirt   just before he reached around
& plucked out a chest hair
he jumped backwards

the man in the gray t-shirt spun around quickly
& rubbed his chest with a clenched fist
he looked riled but grabbed the man with a
mustache & kissed him

they kissed roughly rubbing chin whiskers

they were both buying loaves of bread

& dropped them onto the floor

june smiled

the man standing behind the tongue-suckers
was wearing a silk scarf
& had six green peppers in his hands
he dropped them too

they fell down next to the bread

lee looked at june   june still smiled

the man who had just dropped the peppers
pulled out his penis & shouted   HEY

everyone stopped & looked at him

his penis was large & had two eyeballs . . .
it had feline whiskers

the men who were kissing crouched down
to get a closer look at the penis
the penis meowed like a cat
& the men stood back up

christ!   your penis is a pussycat
said the man with a mustache

it's the most beautiful thing that i have ever seen!
said the man with the chest hair
as he reached out to touch it

the man with the scarf reached down with his hands
covered his penis   & then turned around
DON'T TOUCH IT!   he shouted
if you TOUCH it   i will KILL you

easy   easy   i simply said that it was
the most beautiful thing
please turn back around

yes   please turn back around

i agree   said june   please turn back around

lee still stood by the door trying to ignore the
exhibition as june walked around from behind the
cash register to the front side & joined the men

lee

what june

you gotta come look at this thing

the car is still running

shut it off   do it quickly
before he turns back around

i would rather not

just run   run fast
said the man with the mustache

mind your own fuckin' business
i was talking with june   lee told him

look   i don't want any problems

then mind your own damn business

okay

okay

lee shook his head
& then slowly walked out into the parking lot
he pulled on the handle of his car door   opened it
sat down in the driver's seat
looked at himself in the rear-view mirror
fixed his hair   reached down under the seat
& pulled out a bottle of whiskey
sat it on his lap
& then reached down under the seat once more
this time he pulled out a pistol

lee put the pistol up to his temple
& then pulled it away

he looked at it
& then pressed it against his right cheekbone

he looked into the mirror once again
then pulled the pistol away from his face

strangers were walking around his car
so he tucked the pistol away
pressed under his waistband
covered it with his shirt
picked up the bottle of whiskey   opened it
& finished the bottle before tossing it down

the whiskey made his throat throb

he burped & then looked into the mirror again
before reaching down to turn the engine off
he pulled on the door handle to open it
stepped out   closed the door
then walked back into the store

nobody had moved

they were all still standing in the same places
where they had been standing before lee
walked outside

you're back   june said   come here
we have been waiting for you
you should hear this thing
it has been purring so loud
once i even heard it hiss . . . .

this is stupid

no   lee   this is beautiful

have you completely-fucking-lost your grasp
on beauty?   first you tell me that i am not
beautiful   & now   you are going to try &
convince us all that this man with a pussycat penis
is not beautiful   that his penis is not beautiful . . .
i don't even know you anymore

june   for some damn reason
you have convinced yourself that this world
only likes skinny women
i don't know why this is
& i don't know how you survive
you are eighty-four pounds & over six feet tall
give up already   your size is not beautiful anymore
none of this shit is beautiful

silence!
i'm not turning around unless there is silence!
said the man that everyone was watching

hush . . . said the man with the chest hair

shhhh . . . said the man with the mustache

june looked at lee
& pressed her index finger against her lips

lee stuck his middle finger up & waved it
at all four of them

it was quiet now

are you ready now

uh huh

the man slowly turned back around
& removed his hands to reveal his penis once again
his penis slowly moved its eyeballs up & down
as if it was trying to make eye contact with the
crowd

can i touch it   june asked

lee reached over & pulled june backwards
by the shoulder once she started to move forward

june shrugged her shoulder & pushed lee away

only if you follow my instructions closely
the man said

i will   i will   june said   i promise

okay   the first thing you have to do is kneel down
onto your knees

don't do it   lee said

do it   do it   the other men chanted

june leaned forward & gently fell to her knees
as the man pulled his pants down to his ankles
his whole pubic area was gray & exposed
he lifted his shirt up
tucking it underneath his chin

the second thing that you have to do
is pull your hair away from your face
& hold it with both hands behind your head

how in the world will she ever touch your penis
with her hands behind her head
the man with the chest hair asked

don't do it   lee said again

i'm going to do it lee   just be quiet & watch

june gathered her hair up with her fingers
& held it tightly behind her head

the final thing that you have to do is simply
close your eyes & be very still

june closed her eyes & tensed up all the muscles
in her body   she made a large smile
with her mouth & held it

lee stood there & watched her smile

the man with the pussycat penis watched her smile

the man with the mustache watched her smile

the man with the chest hair watched her smile

they all stood there watching june smile
& everyone except the man with the pussycat penis
was anticipating what was going to happen next

the man reached down & grasped his penis gently
with three fingers   it meowed again
he moved closer towards june's face
& once he was close enough to touch june's ear
with his penis   he stopped & let go of it
his penis started wiggling all by itself
& started to softly nudge june's earlobe

awe . . . the other men whispered as june
continued to remain tense

lee's insides groaned

he likes you lady

awe . . . the men whispered again

he really likes you a lot lady
turn your head towards me
& let me touch him against your lips

june nodded her head
& started to turn towards the penis

the men held hands tightly

& lee pulled his pistol out

get the FUCK up off the floor june

easy   lee   i'm getting up now!

buy your fucking bread & peppers
& get the fuck out of my sight
before i shoot all of you weird son-of-a-bitches

june   ring up their groceries

okay   okay

the man quickly pulled his pants up
& dropped his shirt back down

the other men scrambled to pick up all the bread
& peppers

they threw everything up on the counter
& june pushed the buttons

they all paid & then quickly ran out of sight

lee   june said   what the hell was that all about

i like your smile & your lips

you like them

yes   i like them
they haven't changed at all since i met you
everything else has

so my lips & my smile are still beautiful

yes   june   they are

were you really going to kill those men
were you really going to shoot them

no june   i don't have any bullets for this pistol
so it's not shooting anyone

lee   what would you have done if they didn't leave

who knows   june   who knows

not me lee
but i know that penis was something else
wasn't it beautiful

shut up june

okay lee

lee put his pistol back under his shirt
& burped again
before he said

june
i think we are out of olives & crackers at home
i'll go grab some

VICTOR CLEVENGER spends his days in a Madhouse and his nights writing. Selected pieces of his work have appeared in print magazines and journals around the world. He is the author of several collections of poetry including *Sandpaper Lovin'* (Crisis Chronicles Press, 2017), *A Finger in the Hornets' Nest* (Red Flag Poetry, 2018), *Corned Beef Hash By Candlelight* (Luchador Press, 2019), *A Wildflower In Blood* (Roaring Junior Press, 2020), and *Scratching To Get By* (Between Shadows Press, 2021). Together with American poet John Dorsey, they run a small poetry press called River Dog. He can be reached at: crownofcrows@yahoo.com

Also Available From Anxiety Press

Cialis, Verdi, Gin, Jag by Adam Johnson

Switchboard Rot by Michael Gerard

Song of the Sister by Leia John

Ballad of an American Ganymede: Or, Explorations of Queeritude in Fifty Seven Cantos by G. R. Tomaini

Screw Factory by Edward Anki

Sweat and Blood Between the Cracks by Joe Haward

Homo Mortalis: Meditations on Memento Mori by Sebastian Vice

Tomorrow Everyday, Yesterday Too by Carson Pytell

Blood Honey by David Estringel

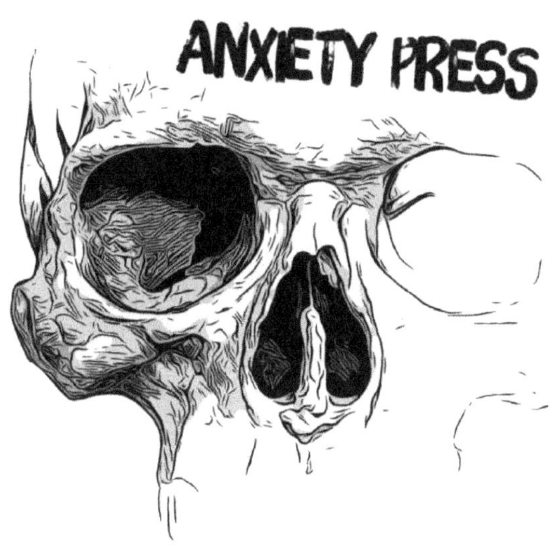
ANXIETY PRESS

DIVINE DOMINATION

EVERLY STONE